The Year We Studied Women

The Year We Studied Women

Bruce Snider

The University of Wisconsin Press

The University of Wisconsin Press
1930 Monroe Street, 3rd floor
Madison, Wisconsin 53711-2059
uwpress.wisc.edu

3 Henrietta Street
London WC2E 8LU, England
eurospanbookstore.com

Printed in the United States of America

Text design by Carol Sawyer of Rose Design

Library of Congress Cataloging-in-Publication Data

Snider, Bruce.
   The year we studied women / Bruce Snider.
       p. cm.—(The Felix Pollak prize in poetry)
   ISBN 0-299-19380-2 (hardcover : alk. paper)
   ISBN 0-299-19384-5 (pbk. : alk. paper)
I. Title. II. Felix Pollak prize in poetry (Series)
PS3619.N53 Y43   2004
811'.6—dc21   2003006270

ISBN-13: 978-0-299-19384-3 (pbk: alk. paper)

for my grandparents,
Helen and Verlie Snider
and for TJ

*The Book of Life begins with a man
and a woman in a garden. It ends with
Revelations.*

—OSCAR WILDE, *A WOMAN OF NO IMPORTANCE*

Contents

Acknowledgments

Many thanks to the following journals in which some of these poems first appeared, often in earlier forms:

Artful Dodge: "Child's Play"
Beacon Street Review: "Physical Education," "Skeletons," "News"
Blue Mesa Review: "Strawberries"
Borderlands: Texas Poetry Review: "Against Nostalgia," "The Variables," "Letter to an Imagined Lover"
Crab Orchard Review: "Wigs and Tanning"
Cream City Review: "Morning"
Gulf Coast: "Aunt Ginny's Birthday Wish"
Hayden's Ferry Review: "Making It Up"
Marlboro Review: "Not an Elegy"
Many Mountains Moving: "Prayer for a Snowy Day"
Mid-American Review: "This Is the Last Poem with the Ocean in It"
Prairie Schooner: "April"
Sycamore Review: "Nostalgia"
The Texas Observer: "Sperm," "The Eagle Tattoo"
Third Coast: "The Certainty of Numbers"
Willow Springs: "The Fat Sister Speaks"

"Making Room" was reprinted in the anthology *Is This Forever, or What? Poems and Paintings from Texas,* published by Greenwillow Books.

I also want to thank several people who supported or contributed in some way to the completion of this book: Amy Adams, Marla Akin, Beth Chapoton and the "2–3" gang, Darin Ciccotelli, Jill Alexander Essbaum, Steve Gehrke, Vivé Griffith, Maria Hong, James Magnuson, Phil Pardi, Steven Rahe, Marcia Southwick, Gloria Tidwell, TJ Wasden, and especially my family.

Special thanks to my teachers: Richard Cecil, Judith Kroll, Cornelia Nixon, Naomi Shihab Nye, Maura Stanton, Laurel Steill, David Wevill, Thomas Whitbread, and David Wojahn.

I also owe an enormous debt of gratitude to James A. Michener and the Michener Center for Writers, who provided the fellowship support and community that made the writing of this book possible.

The Year
We Studied Women

A Drag Queen Is Like a Poem

in the same way that a drag
queen is like a woman
except of course that the woman
has real breasts while the drag queen
unbuttons her blouse
to reveal the *realistic breast form*
for cross dressers she's ordered
like alligator shoes
from the *Gucci* catalog.
But then it's not so much shoes
that matter when talking
about poetry as it is the hair
and jewelry and the way
the lipstick has been applied.
Any teenage girl can tell you
that a good poem needs
to wear a short skirt if she
wants the boys to notice,
and that eye shadow can say
just as much as the subtle shadings
of anything Keats or Eliot
ever wrote. The truth is

it's all about truth
and beauty, or what passes for it,
and so there will always be someone
to argue it doesn't matter
what sprouts between
your legs like so much moss
between the paving stones. You can
always just pad or shave
or powder. You can strap
on foam tits and a rubber ass
to remind yourself that the language
of the body can always
be rewritten, that ultimately poem
is to the poet as drag
is to the queen, each word
fitting together like male
and female, like an infant
and his mother, two bodies,
two hearts, but one
coming out of the other.

It's not the numbers you dislike—
the 3s or 5s or 7s—but the way
the answers leave no room for you,
the way 4 plus 2 is always 6
never 9 or 10 or Florida,
the way 3 divided by 1
is never an essay about spelunking
or poached salmon, which is why
you never seemed to get the answer right
when the Algebra teacher asked,
If a man floating down a river in a canoe
has traveled three miles of a twelve mile canyon
in five minutes, how long will it take him
to complete the race? Which of course depends
on if the wind resistance is 13 miles an hour
and he's traveling upstream
against a 2 mile an hour current
and his arms are tired and he's thinking
about the first time he ever saw Florida,
which was in the seventh grade
right after his parents' divorce
and he felt overshadowed

by the palm trees, neon sun visors,
and cheap postcards swimming
with alligators. Nothing is ever simple,
except for the way the 3 looks like two shells
washed up on last night's shore,
but then sometimes it looks like a bird
gently crushed on its side.
And the 1—once so certain
you could lean up against it
like a gray fence post—has grown weary,
fascinated by the perpetual
itch of its own body.
Even the Algebra teacher
waving his formulas like baseball bats,
pauses occasionally when he tells you
that a 9 and a 2 are traveling in a canoe
on a river in a canyon. How long
will it take them to complete their journey?
That is if they don't lose their oars
and panic and strike the rocks,
shattering the canoe. Nothing is ever certain.
We had no plan, the numbers would tell us,
at the moment of our deaths.

Another Kind of Sword,
Another Kind of Stone

And so it goes in these stories:
a boy and his sword off to slay the dragon

or find love, which is another
kind of sword forced into another

kind of stone. You learn this quickly
when you're the hero. You learn

that stabbing one Dark Overlord
only means another

will take his place. You learn to keep
your hand on your sword, which is magic

and will never fail you,
especially when you cleave

off another man's head. Sometimes
the sword glows when you do this,

sometimes it sings like a small bird
or a radio, like your mother sang to you

as a boy tucked under the covers
on a cold night. But it can't love you

like a mother, even though it draws
blood, even though you'll know

by the first chapter that you're just another
orphan, your destiny just another

kind of sword drawn
from another kind of stone

that is your past. When the minstrels
write your songs, you won't even

recognize that noble brute swimming
the moat, scaling the castle walls.

There's so much left out for sake of rhyme,
for narrative flow (i.e. the fiery sunset,

the calla lilies, the dirt under your nails),
until the song you leave behind

will be the song they made of you,
the song of your sword, its slicing

and dodging, its throwing of dust.
You'll begin and end forever,

with your *once upon a time,*
your *happily ever after,* your song,

which will be their song, too, the song
of the woodsman chopping in the distance,

the song of his axe, of the blade
and the tree, of the falling

and rising as the plank in the house,
the chapel door, the coffin, the page

in the old book, the song of something
opened, something slammed shut.

April

My cousin April unveiled her freckled chest,
the pink nipples like my own, startling me
with our commonness, our bodies that were not yet broken
open, still pink and spongy. At night

under grandma's satiny comforter, we played
Married, lying on top of each other in the dark, a boy
and a girl, like our parents but happier, her small pelvis
against my hip bone making a soft clatter

deep in its socket. In the morning we'd play
Dress Up, draping ourselves with grandma's
nightgowns and jewelry, a sapphire bracelet,
a rhinestone stick pin, strands of pearls,

the sample lipsticks left by the Avon Lady:
Carnation, Starshine Pink, Dusky Rose, ripe tokens
of womanhood worn by a boy and a girl painting
their nails in the kitchen beside the butter knives,

keeping a look out for my father who'd caught us
once, his temper flaring like the rouge on our cheeks.

Boys don't wear makeup, he'd said, so lipstick
became our secret, April powdering my face, April

whose name was spring, whose body was like mine,
unfinished, almost ethereal, thin as the shadow puppets
we made at night in the porch light, all those birds
and wolves coming out of our hands.

.

The Reading

I. The Fool

This card is you, an effeminate youth
on the cliff's edge, clutching a small
white rose. It's something you could've dreamed
if you remembered your dreams.
You imagine they're full of flying

alligators, green balloons and sock puppets,
Abraham Lincoln cartwheeling into your
bedroom with a spider on his face, Bette
Davis brewing you a cup of black coffee,
wearing a bull fighter's cape. *Magritte has nothing*

on me, you say. Secretly, though,
you worry. Most nights your brain's
just white noise on the television
at 3 A.M. Lately, fears circle you
like scrawny dogs leaving puddles

at your feet. You've never liked dogs,
all that hair, that drooling. You're like your father

in that way. He once swerved
to hit a dog when you were just a boy,
but that was no surprise. He also shot dead

five men standing outside
the enemy latrine, ate raw fish
with the eyes still in, slept with whores,
and skinned a live snake with a spoon. Unlike you,
he was capable of anything.

Unlike you, he owned a Bible and said grace
at every meal: *God bless this table, this family,
this tuna noodle casserole.* You could say
a lack of irony was his weakness in the end
as he moved through the world, an astronaut

barreling into the future with his
fancy little space suit and brand
new American flag. Admit it,
you're no different, always dying
to thrust something into the moon.

Who can say what it's really like
up on that dead, shiny stone? Some nights
it breaks through the trees like one
of those geese you hunted with your father,
both of you dressed in fatigues, rifles

slung over shoulders. Some got away,
but then you turned your guns

toward the sloping necks of others
along the riverbank, who stood there right
in front of you, feeding and singing

and feeding.

II. Page of Cups

This is the card that covers you
like the shadow of your father's car
slipping into the driveway
when you're twelve and he's been out all night
again. At that age anything
can seem like an omen,
even him, stumbling across the threshold.
Even his key, swiveling in the lock.
At that age how can you not pity
his sloped shoulders,
then look past them for a sign about yourself?
The next message could come from anywhere, a blazing comet
or another note from the teacher
for your mother to sign,
something about the field trip
to the Plains Indian Museum
or your stolen red gym shoes,
or how you chew your nails
and talk too much. It's all about asking the right
questions, but when you try to answer them,
you find another question
within the question
like a hollow doll within a hollow doll,
which, ultimately, is why you buy
so many self-help books,
most of which say you should open your heart
as if it were like opening your mailbox.
Which you did today.
There were two bills, coupons for free tanning bed sessions,

and another smudged, sorrowful letter
from a distant friend. You tried to read it, but the words
were as indecipherable as the school nurse's signature
on the lice-check forms
she'd hand out each fall.
You can still feel her picking
at your head with her sterile gloves
·as if she were memory
itself, her thick fingers combing
through those dark hairs
in your flawless pink scalp.

III. Ace of Swords

This is the card that crosses you,
the jutting chair leg, the skates you left lying

on the stairs. It's the one bruised
persimmon in the whole basket, the one sail

that won't fill with air. It's the first time
the condom ruptured, the first puncture

wound blossoming in the chest. It's the second wife
to fuck around, the cancer cell

deaf to the weeping at the desk. It's your father
with the belt in his hand, the wise man

who tells you the real problem
isn't that you're in danger, but that you ever

thought you weren't. It's that voice in your head
that keeps crying, *Here you are on stage again,*

not the song but the singer, not the hammer
but the nail.

IV. King of Swords

As snow crowns the mountaintop
        this card crowns

        you, cold as the day you
were born: streets

caked with ice, your father
        hammering some guy

        in a bar across town, you
becoming you as his fist

becomes a weapon, or so
        your mother

        tells you. You've always
wondered what really

happened that day, if
        it was all another game

        like your mother buying
him flowers on her

own birthday because
        he always forgot?

When your father
launched his fist, did

the guy's face crack
        like that vase on

        the kitchen table, did blood
pour from him

the way water pours
        from the vase?

        Did his vision cloud
as water clouds

when the petals begin
        to sag and wilt? Did he

        cry out as your mother
cried out on that day

you passed through her,
        as she still cries out

        years later in her sleep?
Did your father pull

a knife as she claims, or as
        you suspect, did he

say *fuck you,* and swing
again, knowing on the day

you were born
    anything could be

    a weapon, even words
and fists, even a flower, even a son?

V. The Moon

The street lamp shines
behind the liquor store
parking lot where you're sitting

in your father's truck, waiting for him again.
Someone should have warned
you about the light, the way it burns

your eyes, delineating the dark, the way he enters it
like a diver entering cold water
from a great height. It's not exactly clear

when you began to believe
in man's ability to change
for the worse, but it had something to do

with late-night movies, your father
dragging his shadow across the asphalt
like Bela Lugosi dragging a corpse

across the screen. You knew monsters
were self-created (the giant tarantula
born of the scientist's greed, the werewolf

awakened by the school teacher's impatient wife)
but you were just a boy watching TV, a boy
helping his father into a truck. You knew nothing

of evil, only fear, which has no shape
but the shape you give it. You could feel
its foul breath on your neck,

but you knew *it* wasn't the killer
in the movie. If anything it was the making
of the movie: one man yelling *Action!,*

the other entering the killer's room.
One screaming when the razor's
at his throat, the other yelling *Cut!*

VI. Death

This card rests
       beneath you
as the infant rots

       beneath the freshly
cut grass. *2001–2001*
       the stone says, two plots

down from another
       that says nothing,
though it will say, *husband,*

       father, soldier.
On that day
       decay will stop

up his pores like chimney
       flues, his breath nothing
but the embalming

       fluid's song:
you lose, you lose.
       It's that simple,

or is it? When
       he's lying there in rouge
and his Sunday suit,

he won't stop loving you.
Even under
    the white sheet

he'll fall for you
    as snow over pine
forests, each flake

    carved from ache
and bone. Alone,
    you'll sit at the window

watching the shapes
    become him
against your will,

    your grief
another draftsman
    with a hole

to drill, until one day
    you'll be
like him, toughened,

    always unsure, whistling,
using his lucky fishing
    lure, your temper

quick as a rat darting
    from the trash, the damp
flakes falling right

around you,
clumped like tight
white fists, like ash.

VII. The Magician

Now you see it, now you don't:
blue scarves spool out from a black cape,
the past
        you've always known
would one day come back for you
like your father coming back
for your mother after the war, swooning,
scraping hair-thin pieces of shrapnel
from his gut. It had something to do
with love, something to do with cold
sweats and nightmares,
                  the starry face
of a corpse in a mound of new grass.
You can imagine him
standing there at nineteen,
too thin, squinting into the afternoon
light as he steps off
the Greyhound from Missouri, running
a hand over fresh stubs of hair.
He's still clean shaven but the distance
between who he was
            and who he's become
is the distance between what is given
and what is taken away. You could say
the war ruined him. You could say
a lot that isn't true, just sentimental
and naïve. You could say when he was drunk

he'd talk about the minefield's glare
smeared across the sky,

                 about a dead friend
he carried for hours in a swamp. But there
are always more questions
than answers, always more doves
up the magician's sleeve. You can wave
your hands all you want,

                      but will the woman
in the red sequined body suit
really disappear? Will your father really carry
that body for the rest of his life? Will you
really carry it

              for the rest of yours?

VIII. Temperance

As the rifle answers the cries
of the geese, this card
answers you, small thudding
carcasses at your feet.
Your father turns to look at you
with the same unflappable expression.
Don't worry, he says, *we kill them
for their meat.* And suddenly
you'd like to start over.
You'd like to be something
else in this scene, the field maybe,
even the gun. You'd like to be the bullet
in the gun. You'd like to sail through the air
toward explosive release,
to hit something the way you hit
that deaf kid who rode your bus
in the eighth grade. Nothing prepared you
for that kind of pleasure, his blood
spraying the snow, his cries
dissolving into the cold like fog,
simplifying everything. Who knew
you even had it in you, rage
honed so thin it could be the nail
your father drove
to hang your school picture
that year, the same year your parents
split, their wedding photos
staring back like the stuffed heads
of glassy-eyed deer. That was years ago

but even now you could bow
to that deaf kid as the Sioux
bowed to the buffalo
after slitting its throat. You could turn to him
the way your father turns toward these geese
above the trees, the way,
rifle cocked, he turns toward you
as if at any moment he might
vanish the way snow
vanishes, or a fist
when you open your hand.

IX. The Lovers

This card strengthens you, your heart
pumping like pistons in your father's '66 Corvette
as you watch all those couples on park benches,
their lips fused, making you
believe a day might arrive
like no other day, its sky and trees
like no other sky and trees, its dawn
a harsh reconciliation. For example, a boy
might love a man. A father might not speak
to a son. The junior high basketball team
might swing their jock straps, quoting Oscar Wilde
who said, among other things,
There is nothing so difficult to love
as a large nose. Ok, so maybe
they wouldn't quote Oscar Wilde. Maybe
they'd just blush and jerk off in the bathroom,
even the shy ones who make good grades
and eat the cheese sandwiches their mothers
make them for lunch. Unfortunately,
Oscar Wilde said very little about
the importance of a good cheese sandwich.
He was too busy getting it
off with Bosie, who didn't give a shit
about anything and was really just trying
to piss off his father. But that's the thing
about fathers. Some don't say a word
when you're screwing a major literary figure.
Others are like Romeo
wooing Juliet. It's all talk, talk, talk.

Not that fathers are anything like lovers.
Unless of course you consider those dreams
where his hands keep groping wildly, shivers
like small explosions down your spine. *On your knees,*
he says, as if to suggest you're just another woman
watching reruns on Nick at Nite.
One second it's Ricky in his Cuban accent
saying *Lucy, you've got some 'splainin to do,*
the next it's *him* pinning you to the floor.
Sometimes the dream's that confusing. Sometimes
your hands are tied behind your back.
Sometimes you're blindfolded and can't see
his mouth moving, but you can always
hear his words.

X. The Hermit

This is the card that defines you
as the dictionary defines the words

embryo: a vertebrate at any stage of development prior to birth or hatching

lunar: of or relating to the moon

solitude: the quality or state of being alone

which is comforting somehow,
knowing that each word
houses its own meaning
the way a body houses
its own blood, which may,
in fact, be less comforting
when you think about it,
considering how easily blood
spills from its container
of skin, how it can grow
sticky and

clot: to undergo a series of chemical and physical reactions such that fluid is converted into a coagulum

which is what words do,
thickening on your tongue, evolving
like the lizards whose ribs widened
over centuries to become the leathery wings

of the first fruit bat, emerging
like an unsuspecting

father: the male parent

who walks out one day
to find himself changed, unable
to speak the language
of his only

son: a male human being in relation to his parents

until there is nothing to be done
but pour another drink,
finishing crossword puzzles
at the dinner table,
all those silent vowels
and consonants asking questions
like teenage girls wrenching
petals from daisies: *I love you,
I love you not.* What is the answer?

embryo, lunar, solitude?

What are you trying to say?

clot, father, son?

XI. The Hanged Man

This card ends it
as a ringing phone
ends the silent room.

But for what? Nothing
but a disembodied voice,
then click and plaintive

whine. *Hang up,*
you think to yourself, but you
just stand there listening

to the familiar emptiness,
the dial tone humming
in your ear as patiently

as the Dalai Lama who says,
*when the student is ready, the teacher
will appear.* The dial tone

knows all about readiness,
all about that voice
from your past that sneaks up

on you, the collect call
you accept one night
like a vow of poverty, your

old fears coming back
to you, beggars, their hands out,
waiting to be fed. Face it,

you're still twelve and on
that road trip with your
parents, arguing

about scenery, cheap
motels, and potty breaks.
It's no different

than that movie where the man
ties the dog to his car
then accidentally drives off.

That is if you can read the past
as the dog and you
the bumper, or maybe

the past is the bumper and you're
the mangled dog, though
you usually feel like the rope

holding them together, wishing
you were the knife
that cuts them loose.

Not an Elegy

The boy steps down from the bus
with the spelling test in his hand,
the blue-lined paper
wavering like a torn sail
covered with all those words
that can mean so much, words
like *artichoke* and *geography*,
words that can be the defeat of you—
pumpkin, spaghetti, bowling—
words lined up in neat columns
like threats or punishments.
And the boy ready to run up
the driveway and into the house
with his piece of paper
on which an A
has been scrawled so big and red
it crowds out everything else,
so big it's the defeat
of all misery, so red
it could be a small barn
burning at the edge of a field

with all of those words pouring out
of its open doors like horses
galloping, their manes
on fire, their lives
saved in an instant.

Physical Education

That was the year
        we studied women, glossy
diagrams pink as a flushed
        cheek. I traced the slope
of the esophagus
        with my finger, fallopian
tubes flowering
        out as smooth as the ankles
of girls in gym shorts.
        In P.E. we did somersaults
on white mats and I admired
        Sally Neer's small wrists—
narrow white
        stems—but once
when we kissed behind
        the bleachers I imagined
Paul Rafferty pressing
        his lips to my neck,
his breath rapid
        and warm. At night

I labored over underwear
        ads in the Sears
catalog—men
        in Jockey shorts, muscled
thighs, the thin trail
        of hair at the waistline.
I pressed my favorites
        between Silver Surfer comics
until my mother
        found them, my face
coloring like the face
        of that quiet new girl
the day stains bled
        into her gym shorts, red
spots dotting the white
        foam mats. For weeks
I saw those spots
        as if I had shed
them myself, bright as
        maroon blooms
on a cactus, my body
        unfurling another
new petal, another
        bristling spine.

Prayer for a Snowy Day

Even the snow
    can be fashioned
        into a man

        with stone eyes
    and an ordinary mouth
able to say nothing

kind or tender,
    though his arms
        are spread wide

        in welcome,
    the heart
a piece of charcoal

slipped into his chest
    by a boy
        who wanted someone

        to come stand
   with him
this morning

in the cold.
    Some days that's all
      the hope you get.

      Some days you don't
    even get that,
so the day seems a blessing,

falling down around you
     through the stark limbs
       of the poplar trees

      like a prayer
   you've fashioned
into a man

with stone eyes
    and a stranger's touch
      as vaporous

      and gentle
   as snowfall
on your empty, outstretched arms.

Making It Up

Some nights Nana put on old 45s,
songs from the forties & fifties,
        desire & love & heartbreak
                seeping from the phonograph's mouth,
        with nothing to protect herself
but a dab of rouge, the eyebrow
        pencil spiraling out into black-
                smudged wings. She'd demonstrate
        the correct way to work in foundation, spreading
it evenly up along the hair
        & into the neck to avoid lines. She'd uncap
                the lipstick, her face glaring
        like a scar, somehow beautiful
& doomed, her first husband
        an alcoholic & womanizer,
                her second not what she had hoped.
        What can you do then but restore
the face, cosmetics filling the air
        like light through a torn shade?
                Sometimes—if she'd had a vodka tonic—
        she'd make me up, too, blue

eye shadow & frosted coffee lipstick,
          white powder, then stockings, a pearl
                    choker. She'd teach me to waltz,
          Sinatra's silky baritone
drenching the air, a young boy
          & an old woman, painted & faltering,
                    circling the worn armchair
          & fake velvet sofa, everything spooling
into that moment, the future
          nothing, the past an assemblage of silk scarves
                    & rhinestone brooches, her jade
          earrings catching the lamp light,
winking at me, even now,
          with such endless invitation
                    & promise.

Child's Play

With arthritic hands the old man
broke the necks of chickens
and scalded the hogs
with a paste of lye and ash.
He scraped off the hair
with a butter knife,
dipped turkeys in a boiling vat
to peel off the feathers
and sometimes asked the boy
to hold them by their quivering legs.
It was summer. The slaughter house
reeked of dung and flesh.
In the evening beside the black iron
stove, the old man taught the boy
to whistle old German anthems
he'd learned during the war.
He described the gas that settled
into trenches, the men who coughed
their lungs up in chunks.
Sometimes, when the boy asked,
he'd uncover the skin cancer,
dark patches on his neck and underarms.

Schnell, he'd snarl, *Schnell,*
like a German soldier
and the boy would laugh
and imitate—*Schnell, Schnell*—
until it was time
to set up the humidifier,
rinse and wring out their socks,
wash their hands for the next day
when they would once again
cut the jugulars of cows,
string hides over the clothesline,
polish the knives
and mallets until they shone.

Morning

Between the cattails
and an old hawthorn tree,
down where the women gathered
wild strawberries
in the thicket just beyond
the edge of the pond, a child's body
was found floating near dawn
by a fisherman
who'd just said *Good Morning*
to his own son and daughter, *Good Morning*
over a plate of eggs and a slice of dry toast, *Good Morning*
only to find himself standing
in the early sunlight beside the body
of a dead child.
A dragonfly perched on the exposed
throat like a small pendant
his wife might have worn,
convincing him for a moment
it must be a girl, though when he knelt
closer, the narrow hips
and small bruises along the wrists
made him equally certain

it was a boy. The face
lay slightly to one side
like a piece of torn Styrofoam,
eyes partly opened
toward the sky where a cardinal
may or may not have been flying
at that moment.
A dog may or may not
have howled somewhere in the distance
as he noticed the child's small lips, closed
to hide the teeth, clenched
as if to hold back the tongue. *Good Morning,*
it would have said
had the day fulfilled its promise,
had he not found himself on one knee
in the muddy water
at the edge of the pond.
Without thinking
he reached out
to touch the child's hair,
though he would not
include this in his retelling of the story.
He would not describe
skimming over it—running
it through his fingers
like wet grass—not even to his wife,
though she would want to know
every detail, asking again
and again at night
in bed together.
He would keep that for himself,

the hair soft and shiny,
not mossy as you might expect,
but smooth like the water itself,
and later, returning with the other men
who had not found the body themselves
he would think of his own boyhood
as they lifted it
into the air together, the body
extracted like a cloud
from the belly of the pond, rising
then as only a drowned child
can rise.

Fabric

What the lawyers didn't say
was that neither of you
had a choice once you saw how small
he was, once you heard his narrow
shoulders speak to you about the frail
architecture of his rib cage,
about the delicate, finely scooped bowl
of his skull, about how in this life
there are so few chances
to dominate another man,
even a young man like this
who'd probably known a hundred bullies
like you, sporting their father's
army jackets and crooked teeth.
And you knew that,
which is why you were there
that night drinking in a bar
in a place like any other place
where clouds move like shadows
and weakness is a badge
no man wears when he walks
out into the street. And so you never

had a choice. It was either
beat him and leave him by the field
or forget the fabric
of his shirt was as thin
as what separates you
from becoming him. It was either
beat him and leave him by the field
or take him in your arms
and lift him off that fence, take him
and ease him to the frozen earth, take him
and feel his skin against
your skin, your cheek
against his cheek, this young man
you've come to murder
in a field, take him, please
just take him in your arms.

School Dance

Everything was tragedy
then: acne blooming
in the adolescent flowerbed

of your face, another B
in geometry, and you
the only boy on the decoration committee.

The theme, *An Evening
on the Nile,* seemed terribly
exotic despite the papier-mâché

pyramid that swayed every time
the fans switched on.
You stayed up till midnight

the night before trying
to make the King Tut statue
look less like Mrs. Davidson,

the girl's basketball coach,
explaining to Rhonda Curry
that the Nile couldn't be made

of lavender tissue paper
even if it did match her dress.
For weeks you carried

the E encyclopedia around
for research, which was really
just an excuse to study

all the illustrations of bare-chested men
hoisting stones for pyramids
on the Egypt page. Of course,

your mother was convinced
reading the encyclopedia
could only improve your chances

of getting into a good college,
which was all she talked about
anymore, saying the word *college*

with the kind of reverence
she reserved for other
important C words

like *career* or *Jesus Christ*.
Not that you even noticed,
you were so busy fantasizing

about Ben Duncan, the soccer player
with the great calf muscles,
and trying to avoid Sean Stafford

who kept typing out F-A-G
on your own notebook paper
whenever Mrs. Harlow, the typing

teacher, turned her back, confirming
your belief that the world
could be split in two:

places where people make you
feel like shit and *places where you*
just feel like shit for no reason,

both of which could apply
to the school dance. Even
though you arrived early,

the big Sphinx cake
was already softening
under the lights, all that coconut

frosting oozing down the sides
like your own self-confidence
until you found yourself

wondering if this was all
there would ever be, a kind
of emptiness amidst papier-mâché

and wadded-up Kleenex.
But you still got out there
and started dancing

in the middle of the crowd,
moving from one flat foot
to the other, oblivious to everything

inside you that was straining
to break out, all the rage
and beauty you wouldn't see

for years, though it was there
even then, hurtling through you
like a stone thrown

through a window, like the glare
of the towering street lights
that each night flooded

your whole goddamn room.

Strawberries

still make me think of David Freeman,
whom I was not supposed to love though I did
that summer, fearlessly, like a fish with a hook
punched through its lip, my tongue struggling
not to name what would be hated,

David, whose mother studied to be a nun
but who lived down the road from us smoking
Camel cigarettes and drinking rye whiskey from Dixie cups,
David, who gave me comic books and a red bandana
and cried in front of me when his stepfather
called him a little prick.

I loved him as I was not supposed to love him,
the two of us sleeping over at my house every night,
side by side, until once in the middle of August,
I kissed him and he awoke, looking at my mouth
as if it were a cut opening in my face,

David, saying I disgusted him, saying he hated me.
And though I asked him to stay, he walked home
anyway, the night pressing against me

like the burn of an exhaust pipe,
small and blossoming on my wrist.

When I finally slept that night I dreamed
of my brothers and the wild strawberries
we sometimes picked in the fields around our house,
which you could take as a sign of hope if this story
had turned out, in any way, differently.

Wigs and Tanning

Blonde hair rises like pale sea foam in the display window
      where a neon sign
burns its florescent signature—WIGS AND TANNING—across
      the spotted glass.

It's not the most respectable place, but my friend Sarah, six weeks
      into chemo,
isn't looking for respectability, just new hair, what's left of her own
      patched and fuzzy,

draped with a red scarf. In the back, tanning beds
      hum, glowing
through the cracks, fiery as coal-stoked furnaces.
      All human hair,

the saleswoman says, holding up a honey-colored '60s bob,
      but Sarah runs her fingers
through a mass of red ringlets sitting askew on a featureless
      mannequin's head.

Other wigs are clustered on shelves like giant orchids, some curved,
      shell-like, others cascading

waterfalls of hair. Sarah picks a strawberry blonde pageboy and poses
       at the mirror, angular

and bony, though she's still strong, the doctors hopeful,
       her lymph system
gurgling quietly, the hum of the tanning beds like the hum
       of her cells. *My God,*

she says, slipping on a brown overpermed number called "the Alicia,"
       I look like my mother.
The saleswoman mutters something about *golden highlights*
       and slides
one more from behind the counter, this one more modest,
       a dark blonde,
shoulder-length cut that we all know isn't right but might
       do the trick.

At the register, the woman in line behind us smiles at Sarah
       sympathetically,
her own bronzed skin just fresh from tanning, the bed's
       warmth still coming

off her, cells dividing, mitochondria, those tiny fireboxes
       shedding heat,
each one showering us with its bleak radiance. *Do you want
       to wear it out,*

the saleswoman asks, but Sarah shakes her head *no,*
       as if to remain
wholly herself a moment longer. Outside, she straightens
       her red scarf,

the sunlight reducing her to something essential,
          small and hairless,
her fine skin the color of eggshell. She's carrying another
          woman's hair

in a white plastic bag, and though we'll never know
          the woman,
we will know the hair—shiny, soft, all too human—
          which Sarah

holds close to herself like a stray animal she's found in her
          own backyard,
something small and breathing, something wild
          about to be born.

Aunt Ginny's Birthday Wish

There are no stars to-night
But those of memory

—HART CRANE

The fact is we are late
and the ice cream is melted,
or is it that the ice cream is late
and I am melted?
True, I have been melted before,
but that was long ago
and at a time when love
did not seem so ponderous,
fixed here to my throat
like a fake cameo. Daddy said,
Don't be so fast. Leave something
for the boys to imagine,
but the boys had strong arms
and their breath was warm
on your shoulder, could thread you
like a needle on Friday nights
at the old Lion's Club building

alongside the river, sullen boys
in pressed pants, cigarettes
flaring between fingers. I'd sneak out
through the cellar window
and emerge from behind the briars
on my hands and knees, the wind
teasing the hem of my skirt.
Once, when Daddy caught me
he called me an *ornery little bitch,*
but I didn't flinch.
I wasn't like those other girls,
rapping their fingernails
on the pink lampshades.
I had a reputation. I'm not ashamed
to admit it. The night sky
could shine like a blouse
with its pearl buttons
still winking: *Not tonight.*
Who knows about ever.

The Fat Sister Speaks

My father says I'm in my own world.
My mother talks about weddings
and boys. The doctor
says I could get diabetes,
which, I tell him, sounds
like the name of a Greek goddess,
but he's a dim man
in his clean white smock,
his cold stethoscope
clutching his neck like a string
of his own patient's bones.
At home, I sneak three cupcakes
with green sprinkles
to my room where
I imagine myself nibbling
them like an ant, my slender antennae
slicing the air, until my brother Jackie,
the littlest, bursts in to say
Mother wants me
to fold the laundry.
Unlike the others
he has never called me

BUS STOP or DUMB COW.
Still, I put one finger
to my lips to win his silence
and hold out a cupcake.
His eyes go wide,
then uncertain, but he
closes the door, locking it.
Beyond that door the world
is crowded, remorseless,
riddled with blight.
As the littlest, Jackie
understands this as well as I.
We are the biggest
and smallest, sister and brother.
The world could swallow us
anytime it chooses.
When I finally hand him
the cupcake, he swallows it
with the concentration of a magician
trying to pull doves
from a borrowed hat, pausing
for a moment to straighten his tuxedo
or to wink at his sister
in the front row, the same one
he's tried for years
to saw in half.

Another Confessional Poet
Raises Her Hand

I'm the one over here
with her head in the oven,
the one whose heavy
breasts (twin sorrows)
are white as clock faces,
dark hands sweeping them,
marking time, marking me.
The new dress
I've hung in my closet
swings there on its wire hanger,
another poisonous self.
When I slip it on in the morning
its buttons rub against me
like the fingertips of boys
I've known in the backseats
of their father's cars.
I've loved them all,
lost inside my own skin
as the world sprawled
around me, a sideshow
of men in three-piece suits

brandishing pipes
and five o'clock shadows.
They want me to be like the other girls:
small-boned, ghostly,
my hair screwed back in a ponytail.
But don't give me that.
I'm no fool. Look at me.
No hands. No mirrors.
I can make something shiny
out of each fresh pin-prick,
a wet blister swelling
on my sullen thumb.
Watch the thorn etch my skin
with a bright new poem, a tattoo
of some old snake
flicking its forked tongue
at a haze of mosquitoes
droning, still droning,
siphoning the blood.

This Is the Last Poem
with the Ocean in It

but other poems will be written to take its place.
Poems about birds and socks and gasoline engines.
Poems about the size of an elephant's tusk.
Poems starting with the word "Bottle."
Haiku and sonnets and intricate villanelles,
but this is the last poem with the ocean in it.

When it is read, the air will grow still
with the memory of sea foam. Men in the town squares
will bow their heads and mourn its passing.
Mothers with shopping carts will pause
beside the shelves of canned carrots
to whisper a prayer; they'll hold their young closely
in the streets.

Soon, teachers will weep at the gates of the schoolyards
for the children standing with their hands
in their pockets, their sheets of crumpled paper.
Old men in parks and bingo parlors
will reach for the sleeves of old women
whose voices carry the distant sound of the surf.

The truck driver will be left with only his truck,
the criminal with his pointed heart.

The poet will be left comforting the other poems
who will feel smaller now. Poems about clocks
will tick more softly. Poems about love will grow
weakhearted and faint. Poems
about war will yearn less and suffer more.
And the small poems—the ones about thumbnails
and handshakes and motes of dust—
will shudder one morning like mountains,
weary of upholding the sky.

The History of Lipstick

As if it had always existed,
as if it preceded us like the oceans
or the woolly mammoth,
as if it were yet another of the body's extensions—
another veined nose
or stubby finger—somewhere,
even now, women are uncapping
the glistening tubes, making
of their mouths small embers.

Joan of Arc wore it
in the Crusades to keep her
spirits up. Harriet Tubman
greeted each escaping slave
with a bright lip print on the cheek.
Florence Nightingale applied hers
by candlelight, blotting it
on paper even as she dressed
a soldier's wounds.

Beauty's history is marred by nothing
but the impossibility of sustaining

desire, that frayed telephone wire
sparking in the heat.

The teenage girls hanging out
at the Dairy Queen don't know this yet,
with their tight jeans
and pumped-up hair,
their lips' small flames
drawing the firemen
from across the street.
They feel smoldering and untouchable.

They've never met the old piano teacher
who, on her deathbed,
asked the nurse to help her
apply a little color,
the cancer having spilled
into her ovaries and lungs.

Beauty's history is paint and shape,
the body's insistence
on making of itself a canvas.

It's the women and their faces,
their dazzling, unapproachable
faces.

It's a mother preparing for a Saturday night,
her mouth making
a sparse arc, a kiss for hello
and goodbye, her lonely face

rising above the suburb,
above the neighborhood studded with lights.

It's her young son
the poet who watches, touching
the color to his own mouth,
turning his face
so like her own
toward the mirror

to mime a kiss, his pursed lips
the oldest form of seduction, that fatal pink,

that radiant O.

Sperm

Lately I've been thinking of our sperm
in their little cases, waiting
to be called, to bolster
and bloom like mulberry limbs
scraping bedroom windows
in the spring. What would we say to them
if we could, these harbingers of love,
these urgent arguments of desire
who wait inside us gloved
like old women at garden parties?
The past, we might say,
something about nostalgia,
how it makes the present feel bereft,
how as children we scoured the neighborhood
for important things: bottle caps,
tin whistles, charred pieces of wood.
We built things that our fathers
tore down, then we kissed
our mothers on the cheeks.
This was the way it was done,
our fathers' sperm
becoming our brothers

and sisters, becoming us.
One day, they told us, we would
carry on the family name,
ingratiating ourselves like the maple trees,
dispersing our winged seeds
across the lawn. We would stand
like our fathers in greasy trousers,
starting the engines of old Chevys.
We'd slip off our sunglasses,
unbutton our shirt collars,
wink at pretty girls
on the sides of the road.
Pulling out of our fathers'
driveways, we'd light
our cigarettes, smile
and never look back
as if we weren't even sure
where we'd come from
or who might have come from us.

Making Room

My mother envied the small women,
the ones with bones like blades
of grass, bones
blown thin as wine glass stems.
Even their shadows
took up less space on the sidewalk,
making more room
for love. *I've always been big boned,*
she'd say, a testimony
to her genetic misfortune,
a woman in a long line
of women, tall and athletic
with strong hands and shoulders.
She could work for hours in the garden,
bent over the tomatoes
and squash fattening there
beside her in the sun.
And so each summer
the emptying-out began,
a grapefruit half for breakfast,
bowl after bowl of cabbage soup.
With the beautiful

excess of the saints,
my Catholic-reared mother
tried to shed flesh
like the chickens she boiled
for dumplings and broth.
Edgy, her eyes cleaned out,
miraculous and holy,
she'd descend the scales each morning
with her body
a little more defeated.
She'd cling to me, her first-born son,
whose small bones
were strung together
like wind chimes, singing
a love song
of what she wanted
to be, singing
all through the house.

Skeletons

My father and I caught steelhead in the rain,
his broken knuckles over my hand
on the fishing rod
over the water.
He folded and unfolded each finger
painfully,
then cast his line with a snap.

A road led down the mountain
where the thistles bloomed by the river
and a small budding tree crouched
full of peach blossoms.
There, he carved our names into a trunk—
Bruce I, Bruce II—
his blade grinding like an animal's white tooth.

Over a fire he fried the fillets
and drank warm beer from a cracked thermos,
surveyed the ground and declared,
*A hundred years from now
we'll both be dirt,* while the night sky

folded and unfolded, a nest of bats
perched in a tree over our tent.

When I opened the flap and peered out,
I could see the constellations
jostling their yellow bones
through the hickory limbs: Cassiopeia
lifted a great femur and shook it,
Perseus straightened his spine,
Ursula the bear scratched her rib cage
and ambled toward the Big Dipper,
then turned deep into the heart
of the woods, hunting for meat.

News

Such a busy storm, my mother whispers
to herself, carrying a plate of sandwiches,
slices of cheese and olives
to where I sit at the window
watching the snow hiss
past street signs in the dark.
On TV spiders invade a small town.
A mother beats her arms against a wall
knocking spiders off, throws
boiling water on her son
until his skin blisters
and the spiders drop, wilted blooms.
My uncle comes to the door
on a snowmobile with powdered milk,
smoked sausage, cans of beans,
and news that a young girl,
missing in the storm for four days,
has been found in her own backyard,
buried in a drift of snow.
He holds a newspaper in which a red X
marks a drift near a window
where she tried to climb in.

In the photo her mother stands,
cheeks rosy from windburn,
wrapped in scarves against the cold.
How sad, my mother whispers, folding
the newspaper, and we return to our movie
where the woman has barricaded
herself in the basement.
By morning she'll wake to a city
blanketed in spider web.
Upstairs she'll hear the screams
of people. Outside not even
the wind blows. *Shhhh,*
she'll say to no one, *Shhhhhh*

The Eagle Tattoo

Whenever my father hit me
I could see it
along his bicep,
scraping a hooked beak
down the spine
of each feather.
At night it circled our house,
rapped the fogged windowpanes,
perched on the red maples
outside my bedroom
as I clutched
my blanket, hoping
to soothe it
with soda crackers, seeds,
or bits of tuna
left along the window ledge. Soon,
I would lead it inside,
touch its face,
stroke its twisted feet,
the damp clumps
of feathers separating
under my fingers

to expose loose
veined skin, blue vessels
glistening like wet roads
along the ravine,
winding past the creek
and away from here.

No one, but no one knows
when we'll meet
so I sit gathering my doubts
like wet lemons I've seen on trees.
As a child I loved adventure stories, pirates
dueling on the decks
of blazing ships, but tonight
I'm reading about Rimbaud
and the promise of love,
that soft grave. First a letter
to his family, then one to Verlaine:
Why didn't you come when I signaled you
to get off the boat? And the boat sailing.
And the heart opening like an ulcer.
Suddenly it's twenty years later.
He's writing letters
from Harar and Marseilles,
his knee swollen with a tumor
the size of a pumpkin
as he curses his doctors and France,
the damp weather ripe with infection.
His hand cramps:

I have become a skeleton. I frighten people.
The skin is coming off my back because of the bed.
The doctors amputate his leg
and he waits to recover,
then the letters stop.

No one, but no one knows.
Tomorrow I may answer the phone, write a letter,
but tonight on the horizon
hope waves a tattered white sleeve,
and the pirate covers his one good eye,
and the boat sailing,
and from somewhere that voice,
whispering, taunting:
Quick, tell me if I should come to you.

The Variables

In the hand
the pen writes
what is written.
The paper receives,
is sent, then read
or not read
depending on whether
the lover
turns to cut
the rhododendron
blooming from its pot
on the windowsill.

The letter can sit
beside the cut flower
unopened for days.

The rhododendron
can bloom
though it has been cut.

The lover can watch
one or both or neither, depending
on his mood.

Left to dry on the windowsill
the rhododendron
can be placed
in a vase
in the center of the table
full of words.

The rhododendron can be written on
and folded. It can be mailed
and opened. It can be sealed
with a kiss.

The letter can bloom
or, left drying on the windowsill,
be placed in a vase,
trembling on its stem.

Passing the window
each morning
the postman
can see the letter
lying there
in the sunlight,
a fallen comrade,
as he opens
and closes

his mail pouch
like a bag of seed.

Against Nostalgia

Because the small town
you grew up in will color you
the way hair tonic
stains the barber's hands,
you give yourself over to it,
eventually pulling it on
like a rummage-sale shirt,
the kind your gym teacher wore,
frayed and covered in parrots.
Though you'll spend years
trying to forget the names
of streets, the face
of the neighbor woman
who stood in her flapping
house dress, canning beets,
nothing will prepare you
for the sight of cornfields,
for the heart-stabbing
sound of the school bell.
Nothing will keep it
from calling out to you
like the gravestones

across the road trumpeting
their Christian names,
street lights blinking, haloed
in a green mist, your father
still taking his belt
off its nail, your second grade teacher
smoothing out her tan panty hose.
Even on your death bed—
breathing shallowly, trying
to find the right words
to say—your youth will rise
before you like a red stain
on your mother's pale breast
until there's nothing
left to say but
what you've always said,
which sounds more and more
like an apology
and won't ever
ever be enough.

Nostalgia

There are no letters,
just flyers for cheap washing machines,
ethernet lines surging with e-mail,
telephones crackling
like hot grease. Outside,
the postman wanders
past junk shops and paper
stores, listening to the old postcards
hum quietly their messages:
having a great time, Dear Mary,
why don't you write anymore?
Even his hands miss the weight
of ink and paper, the slim
binding of the envelope's glue,
each letter whispering to the other
something essential
about the weather
or the three bright finches
perched on the bird feeder
all last week, which is really a way
of talking about distance
or loneliness, the way it comes to you,

winged and hungry, beating
its yellow breast. Only
the postman knows
that the sky—once framed
by leafy branches—grows dark
as an apple swarmed
with yellow jackets. He can feel
his once young fingers
begin to stiffen
around the slick new catalogues
for telephones and pagers,
remembering the way
he once crossed a porch
with milk bottles
by the door, his own
mother sharpening a pencil
at the kitchen sink,
carving out *Dear Mary,*
I can't wait to see you
again, her small hands
continuing their small work:
writing, erasing, writing, vanishing.

True, My Father Is a Postman

When I write letters
I talk about the weather,
my grandmother talks about the pigs
she butchers with her sister-in-law
on the farm, my mother talks about my father
and how he refuses to talk. True, my father is a postman
but that does not mean he is a letter writer.
A does not always mean B.
Sometimes it is C
or vice versa. If I were to write you
a letter, for example, I would not necessarily
address it to you, though you may be
the intended receiver.
Perhaps I would address it
to myself or to someone
living elsewhere, apart from us both.
Perhaps I would send it to my friend in Singapore
whom I have not spoken to
in three years, and who, upon receiving the letter,
would quickly discover it was written
to someone else. Now, that could be cruel,
especially if it were a love letter.

If I were to write a love letter
I would be certain to address it
to the intended receiver,
but this does not mean
I would make my affections obvious.
On the contrary, I might detail an event
in my life without emotion
or relate a story I read recently
in the newspaper. Perhaps I would
invent the story: *a man and woman*
en route to Las Vegas were killed
when their station wagon struck
a horse-semi on I–70. Only after careful explanation
would a love story begin to unfold—
the man and woman
on their honeymoon,
married after years of separation,
love letters shuttled back and forth
across the sea—but still it is a story
I could tell in a love letter,
and one no doubt I have,
considering that my judgment
in such matters has never been very competent.

Competence, however, has nothing to do
with love letters. Competence has to do
with the mechanics of things. A postman
delivering a love letter can be called competent,
but the writer of the letter cannot.
Which is not to say that my father
is competent. Often he is,

but often he forgets birthdays
or remembers them when they are not.
Often he sings off-key or salts the food
too much when he cooks. Still, he could write a love letter.
He could sit down with pen and paper
and write from his heart
a letter to someone he loves.
He could write, *Dear Son, I love you,*
because a father can write a love letter
to his son, just as a son can write a love letter
to his father.

The Beginning

I begin with this bird, its wings
opening in the dark like curtains
draping the windows of my childhood

bedroom where I slept, often fitfully,
for many years. I begin with its sharp
beak jutting out like arrowheads

I scoured the ground for as a boy, like the tips
of the nurse's cap my mother wore
at the nursing home, the cap that lay

on her dresser most days, heavy
with the scent of talcum. In fact, this bird
could be my mother, perched above me now,

picking nits from her feathers, each one
another reminder of the wrongs
she suffered. It could even be my father

in his black leather coat, bumming
cigarettes on the corner, coughing
and cursing in one startled breath.

It could be the shape of a word
he said to me tenderly once that I
no longer remember, a word that I've lost

now the way I've lost so many things: spoons,
pencils, photographs, which is another thing
this bird could be, a photograph

from a family vacation we took once
to New Mexico where my aunt bought
turquoise bracelets and my uncle gambled

with the Indian minister outside
our motel, where at night they shouted
at each other until the old couple from Arkansas

banged on the wall. But then maybe
the bird's nothing more than the abstract painting
I did in art class that same year, the one

that received the blue ribbon and the trip
to Florida, the one everyone thought was a tree
or a fountain though it could

just have easily been my face
pressed against the window
of my dying cousin's house the summer

his lungs filled with cysts, the summer
the humidifier sang at his bedside all through
the night. I was twelve, but even then I knew

shadows at the foot of my bed could be any
terrible thing, even this bird
staring back at me, even this bird

whose song darkens the air the way the past
tense can darken a sentence, the way fog
can darken a highway until, against all logic,

the lost driver returns to the beginning
as a way, he hopes, of finally
making it through to the end.

The final image of "Temperance" is borrowed from a line of dialogue in Dashiell Hammett's *The Maltese Falcon*.

"Prayer for a Snowy Day" is inspired by Max Garland's poem "For a Johnson County Snowfall."

"Fabric" is addressed to Aaron McKinney and Russell Henderson, who murdered Matthew Shepard in Wyoming in 1998.

The italicized lines in "Letter to an Imagined Lover" are from Rimbaud's letters as translated in Wallace Fowlie's *Rimbaud: Complete Works, Selected Letters*.

The title "This Is the Last Poem with the Ocean in It" is a line from Reginald Shepherd's poem "First Farewell to Antinous."

The first stanza of "The Beginning" is after the first few lines of Larry Levis's poem "South."

"Not an Elegy" is for Amy Adams. "The History of Lipstick" is for Marla Akin. "Physical Education" and "School Dance" are for Steven Rahe. "Making It Up" is in memory of Laverne Schweitzer, 1917–1994.

The Felix Pollak Prize in Poetry

The University of Wisconsin Press Poetry Series
Ronald Wallace, General Editor

Now We're Getting Somewhere • David Clewell
Henry Taylor, Judge, 1994

The Legend of Light • Bob Hicok
Carolyn Kizer, Judge, 1995

Fragments in Us: Recent and Earlier Poems • Dennis Trudell
Philip Levine, Judge, 1996

Don't Explain • Betsy Sholl
Rita Dove, Judge, 1997

Mrs. Dumpty • Chana Bloch
Donald Hall, Judge, 1998

Liver • Charles Harper Webb
Robert Bly, Judge, 1999

Ejo • Derick Burleson
Alicia Ostriker, Judge, 2000

Borrowed Dress • Cathy Colman
Mark Doty, Judge, 2001

Ripe • Roy Jacobstein
Edward Hirsch, Judge, 2002

The Year We Studied Women • Bruce Snider
Kelly Cherry, Judge, 2003